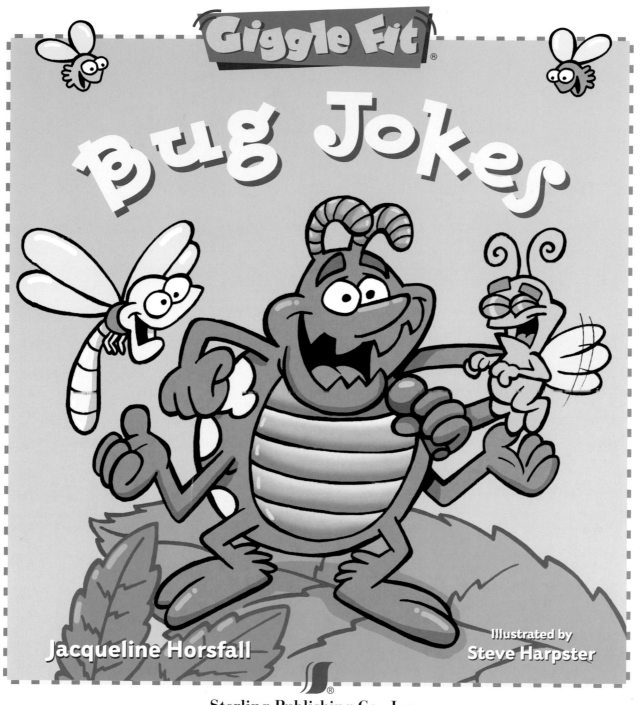

Giggle Fit®

Bug Jokes

Jacqueline Horsfall

Illustrated by
Steve Harpster

Sterling Publishing Co., Inc.
New York

Library of Congress Cataloging-in-Publication Data

Horsfall, Jacqueline.
  Giggle fit : bug jokes / Jacqueline Horsfall ; illustrated by Steve Harpster.
     p. cm.
  ISBN 1-4027-2882-4
  1. Insects—Juvenile humor. 2. Wit and humor, Juvenile. I. Harpster, Steve. II. Title.

PN6231.I56H67 2006
818'.602—dc22

                                            2005019126

10 9 8 7 6 5 4 3 2 1

Published by Sterling Publishing Co., Inc.
387 Park Avenue South, New York, NY 10016
Text © 2006 by Jacqueline Horsfall
Illustrations © 2006 by Steve Harpster
Distributed in Canada by Sterling Publishing
c/o Canadian Manda Group, 165 Dufferin Street
Toronto, Ontario, Canada M6K 3H6
Distributed in the United Kingdom by GMC Distribution Services
Castle Place, 166 High Street, Lewes, East Sussex, England BN7 1XU
Distributed in Australia by Capricorn Link (Australia) Pty. Ltd.
P.O. Box 704, Windsor, NSW 2756, Australia

Sterling ISBN-13: 978-1-4027-2882-2
        ISBN-10: 1-4027-2882-4

For information about custom editions, special sales, premium and
corporate purchases, please contact Sterling Special Sales
Department at 800-805-5489 or specialsales@sterlingpub.com.

How do bugs relax in the tub?
They take buggle baths.

How do horseflies wear their hair?
In ponytails.

Which bugs are very polite?
Ladybugs.

Which bugs live in clocks?
Ticks.

How do you make a tick laugh?
Tickle it.

What kind of bugs live
on dogwood trees?
Bark beetles.

What kind of bugs live on pussy willows?
Caterpillars.

What's a caterpillar's favorite lunch?
A peanut butterfly and jelly sandwich.

What did the apple tree say
to the hungry caterpillar?
"Leaf me alone!"

What do caterpillars play while
spinning their cocoons?
Wrap music.

Why do caterpillars have wrinkled skin?
They're too busy to iron.

Why don't caterpillars have wings?
They like chicken nuggets better.

What do caterpillars wear to
the Cocoon Ball?
Their fur coats.

Why do fleas wear boots?
To walk through poodles.

What did the flea say when
its puppy ran away?
"Doggone!"

Where's the best place to buy fleas?
At a flea market.

What's a flea's favorite plant?
A cattail.

What should you do if there's
a spider in your car?
Take it for a spin.

On what day do spiders
have picnics?
Flyday.

How does a spider greet a fly?
"Very pleased to eat you."

What's a spider's favorite
picnic food?
Corn on the cobweb.

Why are spiders like ducks?
They have webbed feet.

What did the fly say to
the spiderweb?
"I'm stuck on you!"

What did the spider say to the fly?
"Please stick around for dinner."

Why are spiders good at baseball?
They catch lots of flies.

What do you call a spider that didn't take its vitamins?
Daddy Short Legs.

What do you get when you cross Spiderman with a praying mantis?
Spidermantis.

What do you call two spiders on their honeymoon?
Newlywebs.

What would you do if you found a tarantula
in your slipper?
Wear your flip-flops!

What do you get if tarantulas hide
in your strawberry patch?
Very hairy berries.

What are spiders doing on
your computer?
Building websites.

Which juice do tarantulas drink?
Apple spider.

What do you call a jet full of tarantulas?
A scareplane.

What's a tarantula's favorite dessert?
I scream.

What happens when you
put butter on a moth?
Butter fly.

Why did the butterfly cry?
It saw the moth bawl.

Why can't butterflies play volleyball?
They're afraid of the net.

Where do moths go to
dance?
The Moth Ball.

Why do mosquitoes have suckers?
Their candy bars melted.

What carries a sucker and
bounces up and down?
**A mosquito with the
hiccups.**

How can you tell
mosquitoes are tame?
**They eat right out
of your hand.**

What should you do if your
pet mosquito is hungry?
Take it out for a bite.

What do you call a mosquito at the North Pole?
Lost.

What happens when a girl mosquito
meets a boy mosquito?
It's love at first bite.

How do mosquitoes travel?
They itch-hike.

What's a mosquito's favorite sport?
Skin diving.

What do mosquitoes learn in art class?
How to draw blood.

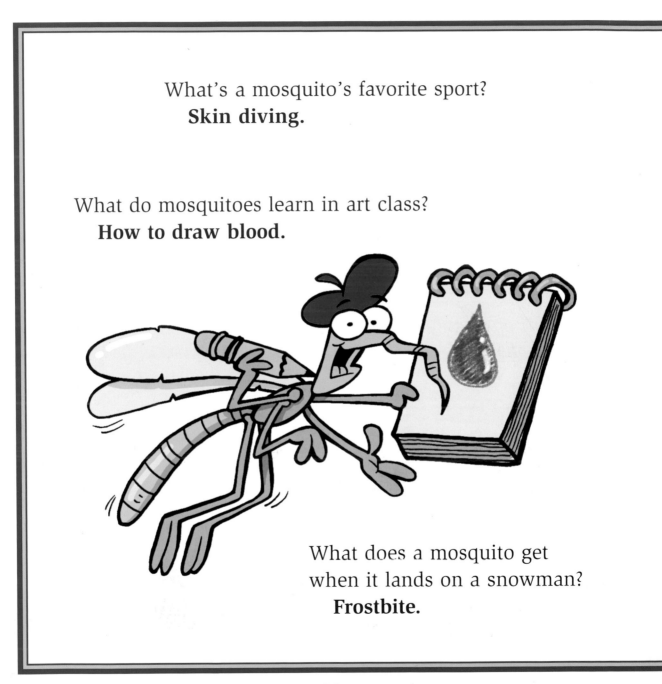

What does a mosquito get
when it lands on a snowman?
Frostbite.

How large is a centipede?
One hundred feet long.

Why can't centipedes skateboard?
They can't find one hundred kneepads.

What do centipedes eat for breakfast?
Scrambled legs.

Why are centipedes terrible dancers?
They have fifty left feet.

What happens when ants picnic
on top of volcanoes?
They have a blast.

Why do flies and ants never work?
They're always at picnics.

Who take ants on vacation?
Uncles.

Where do ants watch football?
At the Sugar Bowl.

What's the best animal to take on a picnic?
An anteater.

Why are ants small and black?
**If they were big and black,
they'd be bowling balls.**

What game do elephants play with ants?
Squash!

Why can't grasshoppers go swimming?
The elephants have all the trunks.

What do you call a bug that jumps in your lemonade?
A glasshopper.

How do sleepy grasshoppers cut their grass?
With yawnmowers.

How do sleepy grasshoppers hop?
They hitch rides on rabbits.

What do grasshoppers wish you on January 1st?
"Hoppy New Year!"

What do you get when you cross
a snake with a grasshopper?
A jump rope.

Where does a grasshopper
fill up?
At the grass station.

Why are grasshoppers good gardeners?
They have green thumbs.

Why should you eat grasshoppers and frogs?
Green things are good for you.

Why don't crickets take
ballet lessons?
They're just tutu small.

Which bug crows at sunrise?
A cockroach.

How can you tell if a cockroach has been at the movies?
By the popcorn stuck in its teeth.

What's the easiest way to catch a cockroach?
Have someone throw it to you.

Why don't cockroaches make reservations at nice hotels?
They like the crumby places.

When do flies celebrate with a big meal?
Garbage day.

Why do flies chase garbage trucks?
They love fast food.

What should you do if a fly lands
on your pepperoni?
Give it a pizza your mind.

How do flies get their
groceries home?
In garbage bags.

Why are flies good at
chores?
**They love to take
out the trash.**

What should you do if a fly
lands on your sandwich?
Read it a breadtime story.

What do you ask a fly
on your bagel?
"Butter, fly?"

What did the fly do when it fell into a bowl
of chicken soup?
Used its noodle.

Why was the fly sitting on a marshmallow?
So it wouldn't fall into the hot chocolate.

Why do flies take so many baths?
They have sticky feet.

What has four legs and flies?
A picnic table.

What's a frog's favorite snack?
French flies.

Why are flies so sweet?
They're always in the sugar bowl.

Should you shoo flies?
No, let them go barefoot.

Why did the fly fall into the mustard?
It couldn't ketchup with the ants.

What did the frog say to the
fly that got away?
"Catch you later!"

What do you get if you cross a hippo with a fly?
**I don't know, but you need a tennis racket
to swat it.**

What's a potato bug's favorite class?
Mashematics.

Why did the stinkbug call the restaurant?
To place his odor.

How do you stop a
stinkbug from smelling?
Hold its nose.

Do sand flies like the beach?
They shore do.

What vehicle do bees drive?
A Hummer.

What does Mr. Bee
call his wife?
Honey.

What does Mrs. Bee tell her husband?
"Hive got a crush on you."

What did Miss Bumblebee
wear to the beach?
Her beekini.

What music do baby
bees like?
A bee CD.

How do bees blow bubbles?
With bumble gum.

How do wasps send messages on their computers?
By bee-mail.

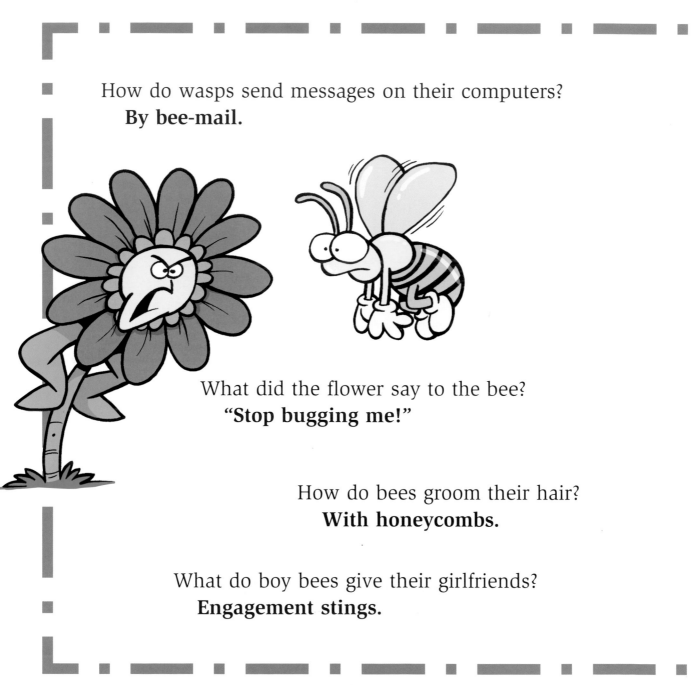

What did the flower say to the bee?
"Stop bugging me!"

How do bees groom their hair?
With honeycombs.

What do boy bees give their girlfriends?
Engagement stings.

Which bug is smarter than a talking parrot?
A spelling bee.

How do little bees get to school?
On the school buzz.

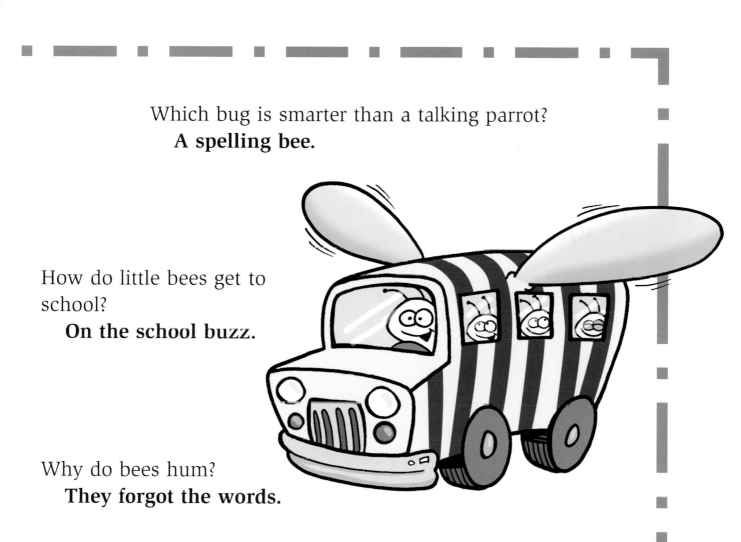

Why do bees hum?
They forgot the words.

Why can't bees say their bedtime prayers?
Their knees are covered with pollen.

What should you do if you get a B on your math test?
Watch that it doesn't sting you.

Why don't bees use the playground?
They're too buzzy.

Why do bumblebees have stripes?
They'd look silly in polka dots.

What goes "Hum-choo! Hum-choo!"?
A bee with a bad cold.

What should you do at a bumblebee's front door?
Press the buzzer.

What did the honeybee say to the rose?
"What time do you open up?"

What do bees wear to dinner?
Yellow jackets.

What did the spider say to the bee?
"Your honey or your life!"

How do grasshoppers begin exercising?
With jumping jacks.

How do bees begin exercising?
With swarm-ups.

What do termites eat in the school cafeteria?
The lunch tables.

What's the best exercise to do while eating chocolate-covered ants?
Crunches.

How do termites travel?
On chew-chew trains.

Where do sleepy termites go?
To the slumberyard.

How would you find beetle eggs?
Go on an eggspedition.

What do termites think about your house?
It's totally gnawsome.

What did the termite say to the house?
"It's been nice gnawing you!"

What do you get when you cross a praying mantis with a termite?
A bug that says grace before eating your house.

What do beetles do when they're in trouble?
Call 911 on their shell phones.

Why do beetles paint their shells red, blue, green, and yellow?
So they can hide in a jar of jelly beans.

What do beetles walk their babies in?
Buggies.

How does a dragon get to school when it misses the bus?

Dragonfly.

What should you do if you find a scorpion in your bathtub?

Pull out the plug!

What takes a month to deliver your letters?

The snailman.

Why are snails so tired?
They carry their homes on their backs.

What do slugs watch at night?
Slime time TV.

Why did the snail cross the road?
It was the chicken's day off.

Why didn't Miss Slug make mud pies in the garden?
She just had her snails done.

How do you start a firefly race?
"Ready . . . set . . . GLOW!"

What do fireflies eat?
Light snacks.

Why do all fireflies go to college?
They're very bright.

How do fireflies say goodbye?
"Gotta glow now!"

What did the fruit fly say to the orange?
"Juicy my banana around here?"

What did the banana do
when it saw a fruit fly?
The banana split.

What did the lemon say
to the fruit fly?
**"Scram, you little
squirt!"**

Why do worms sleep late?
So the early birds won't catch them.

Why do fish eat worms?
They're hooked on them.

What did one worm say to the other?
"There's something very fishy going on here."

What did the worm say to the big pile of leaves?
"**Thank you very mulch.**"

What do you get if you cross a worm with an elephant?
Very big holes in your garden.

What did Mama Worm say when her lost baby returned home?
"**Where in earth have you been?**"

Do worms like carrots?
No, they don't carrot all for them.

Why do baby robins cry?
You'd cry too if you ate worms all day.

Who should you call if your tire blows out?
A flatworm.

What comes after a mayfly?
A June bug.

Which insects are always asleep?
Bedbugs.

What jobs do bedbugs have?
Undercover agents.

What kind of creatures eat
bugs off your car?
Windshield vipers.

What kind of bread do
gnats eat?
Gnatural whole wheat.

How can you avoid biting insects?
Keep your mouth closed.

Index